ALELUYA

Singing the Church Year

*September 2012
To Barbara & Walt,
Corean Bakke*

Corean Bakke

Published by

Bakken Books

Acme, Washington

Copyright © 2010 by Corean Bakke

All rights reserved. No part of this publication may be reproduced, stored in a retrieval system, or transmitted, in any form or by any means, electronic, mechanical, photocopying, recording, or otherwise without the prior permission of Bakken Books.

Scripture quotations marked (CEV) are from the Contemporary English Version © 1991, 1992, 1995 by American Bible Society, Used by Permission.

Permissions note: prompt arrangements can be made for permission for a church congregation to reproduce single hymns for service use, as well as for the wider use of the copyrighted material in this book. Usage fees will apply, please see our website for more information. To obtain permission write to the address below.

Published by:
Bakken Books
PO Box 157
Acme, WA 98220
www.bakkenbooks.com
andrea@bakkenbooks.com

Fabric collage: Corean Bakke
Cover design: Greg Pearson
Editor: Tony Payne
Illustrator: Woody Bakke

ISBN: 978-0-9755345-2-6

CONTENTS

Cover Story   1

Appreciation   3

Author   5

Editor   8

Explanations   10

Hymns with Stories

   Advent

      Jesus Christ, We Sing to You   12
      The Breath of My Life   16

   Christmas

      Rome Gave Orders   20
      Play Your Drum   26

   Epiphany

      Discovery Penetrates Darkness   30
      The People Who Walked in Darkness   34

Lent

    Does Anybody Care 38
    Lament 42
    Can Anything Separate Us 46

Easter

    At Dawn They Came 50
    Aleluya 54

Pentecost

    Do Not Leave This Place 58
    Comforting, Encouraging 62
    Holy Spirit, Come to This Place 66
    God Creator Fashioned Beauty 70
    Once in the Village of Nazareth 74
    When Will Jesus Come 78

Indexes

    Scripture Index 84
    Seasonal Index 88
    Title Index 89
    Tune Index 90

COVER STORY

The fabric collage, designed for the cover, includes all the colors used in my home throughout the Church Year.

> Purple, pink, and blue for Advent
> Red for Christmas
> Orange for Epiphany
> Black for Lent
> White for Easter
> Light green, dark green, and brown for Pentecost

In the spirit of creativity and practicality, I use the traditional colors of the liturgical year as a starting point and then venture beyond with additions and alternatives. All of these colors have become traditions in my home where each season has a distinct focus and identity. It is therefore fitting that each season has its own distinct color.

My grouping of three colors for Advent combines purple, a former color for the season, with the current blue at my parish, and the pink of a single candle in the Advent wreath.

Red is the cultural color for Christmas in this country. I cannot imagine that season without that color.

Orange is my color to symbolize the light in the sky that compelled curious astrologers to investigate, and to symbolize personal moments of profound insight.

The three colors for Pentecost are a deliberate effort to reflect stages of growth throughout these six months – beginning with the color of new growth for June and July, progressing to the color of mature growth in August and September, and ending with earthy shades of brown at the end of the growing season in October and November.

My Lenten color, black, is represented in this collage with threads that make random appearances in each season, with one exception. Easter is not transgressed with black. God wins! Death and evil are conquered!

Aleluya!

APPRECIATION

Chris Berry, Lutheran Campus Pastor at Western Washington University in Bellingham, inspired me to write my first hymn. Six years later, I have sixteen entries for this little hymnal. He requested that a story be written to accompany each of the hymns. Repeatedly I have thanked him for opening a door of creativity that I had never considered entering. His response: "That's what pastors are for!"

Dr. Donald P. Hustad chaired the sacred music department at Moody Bible Institute when I enrolled as a student. Over the years we have become friends. A consummate church musician and editor of numerous hymnals, he has been as a mentor to me. He answered many questions as I faced the challenges of combining text and tune effectively.

Tony Payne and I met twenty-one years ago over a hymnal project when we raced against time gathering songs in nine languages for use at Lausanne II in Manila. He directs special programs and the Artist Series at Wheaton Conservatory of Music and is a prolific composer. He accepted the invitation to transform my hymns from incomplete computerized attempts and handwritten copies into book-worthy pages for this hymnal.

Carolyn Oltman, friend in my church in Bellingham, gave me suggestions and encouragement when I wandered into the world of visual art and needed a professional critique of my cover design.

My son, Woody Bakke, sketched the antique spinning wheel. He is on the faculty of Oak Harbor High School, Whidbey Island, Washington, where he works with students in special education.

A neighbor, Joan Haner, took charge of the proofreading. She is a gift to me in many ways.

Greg Pearson, family friend and graphic designer, photographed my fabric collage and designed the cover. This makes the fourth cover he has designed for Bakken Books.

Andrea Bakke, daughter-in law and business partner, took the manuscript from my hands and made it into a book. With this hymnal, she has pursued all the business steps needed to get four books from computer to printer and ready for distribution. She manages our web site: www.bakkenbooks.com.

Ray Bakke, my husband, supported my hymns with enthusiasm and his clear tenor voice as they were sung at Our Saviour's Lutheran Church and introduced at our monthly Vespers at Bakken. He has been an essential member of the team that brings this book to reality. Financier for this new publication, he will now become publicist.

My thanks go to each of you for your role in making this hymnbook possible.

Corean Bakke

AUTHOR

On Pentecost Sunday in 2000, my husband and I made a dramatic change. We left Chicago, where we raised our sons and took turns completing our formal education, and moved to Acme, Washington. For Ray, it was a return to where he had grown up.

For me, it was like beginning a new career and a new adventure. Many decisions had to be made about what to bring and what to leave behind. I debated the antique spinning wheel, a gift from a Swedish pastor friend. Though in good working condition, I had never used it. Since I expect furnishings to earn their keep, how could I rationalize bringing it? Finally, the thought came: My life in the new location will not be the same. I should take the spinning wheel to symbolize surprises and changes that lay ahead.

I had never written hymns of any consequence. Hymns composed for classroom assignments at Moody Bible Institute always ended in the wastebasket. Because of my interest in hymns, I developed a large collection of hymnals gathered from all over the world. My quest for a church home finally brought me to a Lutheran church, a choice that furthered my interest in hymns.

In 2004 I was invited to write an Easter hymn. The enthusiastic response in my Lutheran congregation motivated me to continue. This book contains the music that followed: a collection of hymns for each season of the Church Year. I have written all the music and words excepting biblical texts.

Vespers at Bakken has been another venue for these hymns. For the past five years, Ray and I have hosted gatherings at our home on the first Sunday of the month, September through May. The format includes music, singing, homily, and prayers. Friends bring friends and my songs are sung.

The words in my compositions do not rhyme. I am not a poet but a storyteller. Each song is introduced by a story. Some of the songs retell stories found in Scripture. I call my musical version of biblical stories *narrative hymns.*

The spinning wheel's silent reminder of surprises has come true. Publication of these hymns marks the tenth year of living in my husband's childhood environment.

Corean Bakke
Pentecost Season 2010

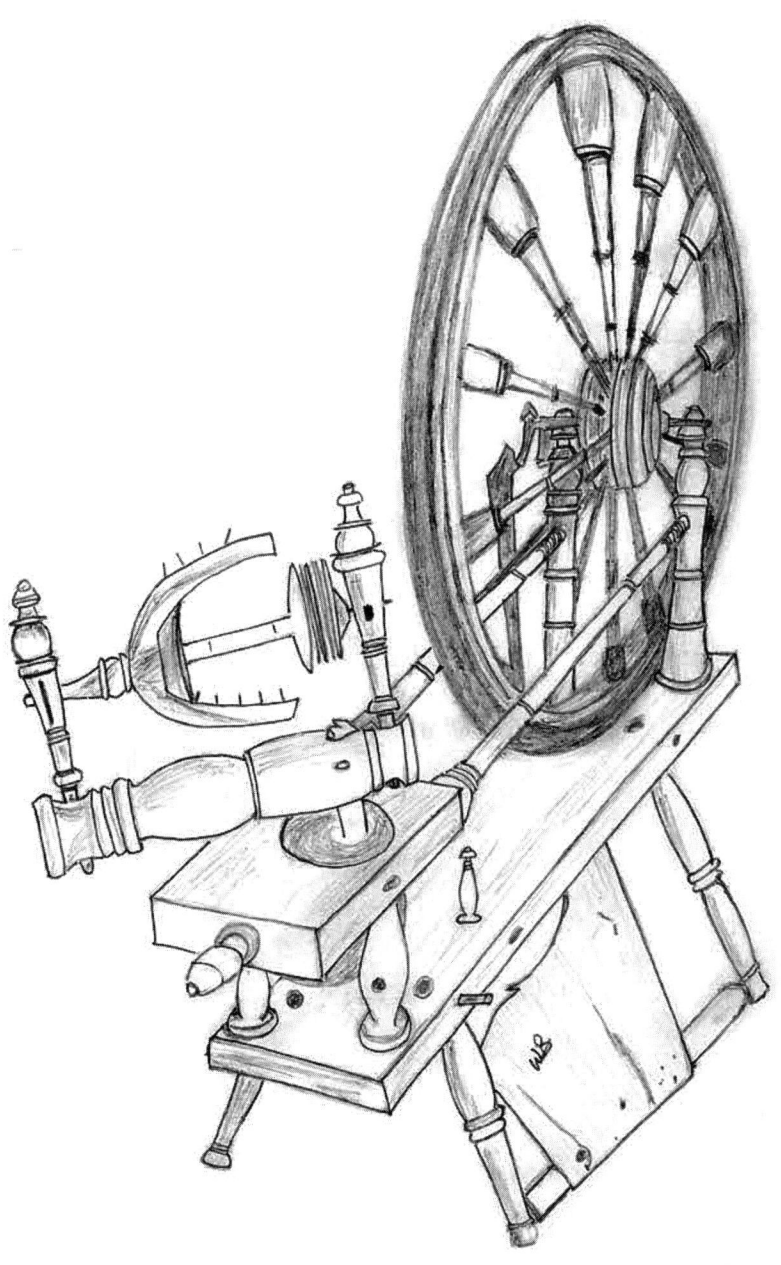

EDITOR

This little jewel of a hymnbook represents a fifth collaboration with my friend and colleague Corean Bakke. With our first collaboration we were pioneers – stitching, cutting and pasting *Aleluya: The Music of Lausanne II*. We did this when computer programs for music writing and graphic layout were in their infancy. Five years later, we improved, expanded and reprinted *Aleluya* and also included it in Corean's book of stories about the music of Lausanne II: *Let The Whole World Sing*. Imitation is the highest form of flattery, which may explain why so many of the songs found in *Aleluya* were later published in other hymnbooks.

Together, we prepared *Aleluya: The Songs of Renewal,* for an American Baptist conference on evangelism held in Washington, D.C.

I consider our latest collaboration, *Aleluya: Singing the Church Year,* a crowning achievement in Corean's long, fruitful, spiritual journey. I have heard it said, "Never get so busy making a living that you fail to make a life." Corean has made a life – a life that is all her own, but poured out for her beloved husband Ray, children and grandchildren, and friends. I am honored to be counted her friend.

You will find no fluff and no rhymes in this book. Instead, you are offered deep gospel truths and prophetic wisdom. I urge you to open your heart to the simple, often sparse melodies and wise words.

I am frequently presented with gifts of relationships that are undeserved. I do not know why Corean and I were drawn together in the tether of friendship for these many years, but I am certainly all the richer for it.

Let the Spirit converse with you as you sing through *Aleluya: Singing the Church Year.*

Tony Payne
Editor & Engraver
Wheaton, Illinois
June 2010

EXPLANATIONS

I grew up with song leaders standing in front of the congregation, directing with hand and arm motions. The accompanying instruments were to support the singing. Not until becoming Lutheran did I encounter congregational singing led by organ or piano.

Not until experiencing Taize prayer services[1] did I learn the strategic role of cantors – proficient singers with strong voices who led congregational song. The instrumentalist played through the song first (Taize songs[2] are short), then lightly continued as the cantor sang. This layered introduction for the congregation not only prepared people for learning new songs quickly, it created an environment for prayer.

The songs of *Aleluya: Singing the Church Year* call for the participation of piano, organ or keyboard, a cantor and congregation. A church filled with worshipers, and homes filled with guests are sizeable congregations. A few family members or friends gathered to sing is a mini-congregation. In each case, a person should be selected to be cantor.

(1) Some songs begin with refrains that may be sung by the cantor alone first, and then repeated with the congregation before continuing into the

---

[1] Taize is a village in Burgundy, France. It became the site of extraordinary gatherings of youth following WWII. Their simple prayer services have been duplicated around the world.

[2] Jacques Berthier composed simple, short worship songs (originally in Latin) for Taize prayer services. Many of them have been translated into English and are used in the US.

verses. This format of listening before singing, even when a song becomes well known, contributes to the prayerful atmosphere.

(2) Some songs are divided between parts for cantor and parts for congregation. The cantor sings such parts alone and then motions for participation of the congregational parts.

(3) One song is written for three sets of participants: cantor, choir, and congregation. "Do Not Leave This Place" tells the story of the coming of the Holy Spirit. The cantor begins. The choir continues the narrative. The congregation sings the refrain, bringing closure to the first verse. The participants move into verse two in the same order: cantor, choir, and congregation. This continues throughout the five verses. In a home setting, the choir part can be sung by a mixed quartet, a trio or a duet.

The final song in this collection was written for *a cappella* choir with the women asking questions as they sing in unison. The men answer as they sing in unison. In the last verse they trade roles and finally join together. A simple accompaniment is included for occasions when singers need instrumental support. Informal groups, including family or friends gathered around the piano, can sing this song.

Jesus Christ, We Sing to You

After writing two hymns, for Easter and Pentecost, I wanted to try writing an Advent hymn. My journal entry for 26 September 2005 describes: "Writing four verses on a topic is much harder for me than verses on a story." With no extended story to follow, as with the first two hymns, I was forced to gather ideas.

On that beautiful, warm autumn day, I put on my big sun hat, made a cup of tea, and sat outside on the wooden bench in our alpine garden with paper and pencil to plan an Advent hymn. My first decision: it should have four verses. Advent includes four Sundays.

In search of ideas, I thought about things happening near and far.

In April I was elected to the pastoral search committee at my Lutheran church and became the chairperson. In May we prepared questions to ask the candidates. In July we conducted practice interviews, using our carefully worded questions. In August we began interviewing candidates given us by the bishop. Another (the third) interim pastor came, committed to stay with us for as long as the pastoral search would take. Patience was wearing thin in the congregation and in the committee.

In August I had watched television in horror as New Orleans filled with water, forcing people onto the ridges of their houses. Boats went from house to house and helicopters rescued from overhead. Hurricane Katrina continued to fill the news.

Verse one would be about both Advents: Christ's humble coming as a baby; Christ's eventual coming as powerful King of the universe. Verse two would be about the search for a pastor. Verse three would be about disaster. Verse four would link Bellingham with Bethlehem.

During the past five years this hymn has been sung by the congregation with organ accompaniment, sung *a cappella* by the choir, and played by handbells. It has also served as the basis for mid-week Advent studies with theme, Scriptures, and discussion questions.

This Advent hymn has taken on a life of its own, exceeding my expectations.

Jesus Christ, We Sing to You

Tune: *Katrina*

Words & Music copyright © 2010 Corean Bakke
All rights reserved. Admin. Bakken Books.

The Breath Of My Life

Mary's song of praise, Luke 1:46-55, is known as the Magnificat. This derives from the first few words: "My soul magnifies the Lord."

The Authorized Version (commonly called King James Version), translated in 1611, used that wording. The Revised Standard Version of 1952 retained those words, as did the New Revised Standard Version of 1989. Whenever my Lutheran congregation hears the Magnificat, it is from the NRSV, which uses the original English wording.

Other translations updated that wording. In checking translations available in my library, I found word changes in The New American Bible and The New English Bible of 1970, the New International Version of 1973, and the Contemporary English Version of 1995.

Christopher Berry, Lutheran Campus Pastor at Western Washington University, prepared a new translation in 2006, working from Greek, Syriac, and Aramaic manuscripts. By working independently of any restrictions, he was free to make a literal translation and to dispense with traditional language.

Chris gave me a copy of his new translation, suggesting that it be set to music. I wrote a piece for organ and *a cappella* choir. The Whatcom Chorale, directed by Charles Peterson, performed it in Bellingham at its annual Christmas concert in 2007. Chris and I attended both performances. My birthday fell on the day before the concert. My gift that year was hearing my setting of the Magnificat directed by a friend from college days in Chicago. That entire Sunday – from beginning to end – felt like a party.

But not everyone shared this enthusiasm for Chris' new translation. Criticism came from those who, while they admired the translation, were appalled by his daring to meddle with the traditional wording of this revered biblical text.

The new translation was as a breath of fresh air for me. For the first time I felt as though I was reading words spoken (or sung) by a young girl, not words of sophistication by an elegantly spoken woman of class.

When my first attempt to write a Christmas carol proved too difficult, I turned to this new translation. Wanting to concentrate on the words that are universal for all people, I selected three lines for the congregation to sing as a refrain. The cantor sings selected pairs of lines that describe God's justness in ruling the world evenhandedly.

The Breath of My Life

Words: Luke 1:47-53 Trans. by Christopher D. Berry
Music: Corean Bakke

Words copyright © 2006 Rev. Christopher D. Berry. Used by permission.
Music copyright © 2010 Corean Bakke. All rights reserved.
Admin. Bakken Books.

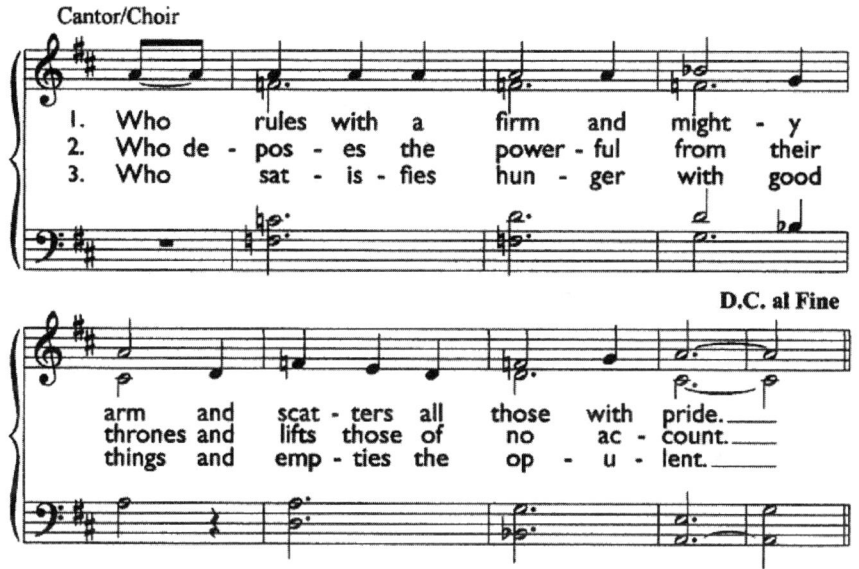

Rome Gave Orders

An extended family Christmas approached. I had volunteered to plan the Christmas Eve worship. It would include people of all ages. Using the format for Lessons and Carols, I compiled a set of Nativity readings from Luke and Matthew that recognized every aspect of the story.

> Roman census
> Joseph and Mary travel to Bethlehem where she gives birth
> Angels tell the shepherds to go find the Child
> Child is named
> Temple in Jerusalem
> Simeon sees the Child
> Anna sees and spreads the word
> Wise men ask directions
> King Herod gets involved
> Escape to Egypt
> Safe return to Nazareth

According to the traditional format of this service, an appropriate carol follows each Scripture. However, I soon learned that parts of the story had never captured the attention of poets and songwriters. Only by selecting single verses from carols, and in one case using a non-Christmas hymn, was I successful in finding something to sing following each reading.

A song that included all parts of the story would have been ideal for concluding this worship. I wished aloud about this to my husband. His reply: "Write one." My response: "There isn't time!"

The next morning, as I lay in bed thinking about the problem, words came to mind along with a melody:

> Who made trouble for Jesus
>   when he was a boy?
> Old King Herod hated him,
>   tried to have him killed.

The melody of the fourth line descended with an augmented second to the last note, giving it the sound of Jewish folk music. Throughout the day, verse followed verse as each part of the Nativity story took on the necessary metric form. When all eleven verses were completed, I added a final summary verse.

The impossible had happened. I had a twelve-verse song ready for the family to sing at the end of our Christmas Eve Lessons and Carols.

Rome Gave Orders

1. Rome gave orders to travel and to pay a tax. All must go to their home town. Caesar had decreed.
2. Joseph traveled with Mary, soon to bear a child. She gave birth in Bethlehem in a cattle stall.
3. Shepherds watching their sheep saw angels in the sky praising God and telling them, "Go and find the child."
4. What will Mary and Joseph name this newborn child? Gabriel the angel said, "Jesus is his name."
5. To the temple they took him in Jerusalem. Jewish law commanded they give him to the Lord.

Tune: *Herod*

Words & Music copyright © 2008 Corean Bakke
All rights reserved. Admin. Bakken Books.

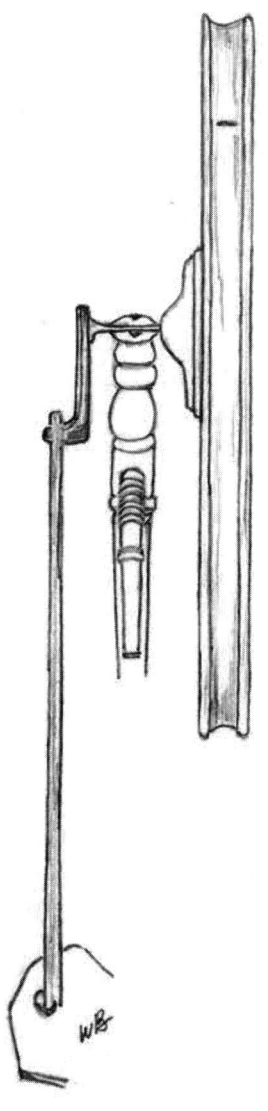

Footman, Left Maiden and Fly Wheel

Play Your Drum

The desire to write a carol for Christmas required some research. Finding the *Oxford Book of Carols*[3] handy on my bookshelf, I began reading the preface:

> Carols are songs with a religious impulse that are simple, hilarious, popular, and modern.
>
> The early carol derived from folk dance and perpetuated folk values of simplicity, humor, and immediate appeal, using down-to-earth language.

Expectations for the text were already in hand. I wanted to write a carol that could relate to people in desperate circumstances. Stories of horrors taking place, especially to women in the Democratic Republic of Congo, played over and over in my mind. None of the traditional Christmas songs that I would be singing seemed relevant to their circumstances. Had the season of joy nothing for them?

With Africa already in my thoughts, memories of reading about the strategic function of drums in primitive African cultures came to mind. Drums conveyed news from village to village.

The final phrase of the refrain, "Come dance with me," brought this carol into compliance with the requirement for hilarity. I always wanted to dance. My parents never allowed dancing. Had they removed Psalm 150 from their Bibles? What if their dream to

---

[3] *The Oxford Book of Carols*, first published 1928, Oxford University Press, London, 1964, p. v.

minister in Africa had come true? Would they have banned dancing there as well?

> Praise God in his sanctuary . . .
> Praise him with tambourine and dance . . .

The word *peace* – used often on Christmas cards – hardly extends beyond the word printed on velvety paper, on glossy red paper, on spotless white paper. I wanted it to embrace people struggling in horrendous circumstances, especially the physically and emotionally brutalized women of Congo.

Joy is my descriptive word for the season. With the shepherds and wise men, we worship the marvelous coming.

The last verse includes seasonal practices of celebration and feasting and the angels' words to Mary and the shepherds, to not be afraid.

To women of Congo at this Christmas season, my drum beats for you, spreading the words: "Be not afraid! God is with you."

Let's dance together!

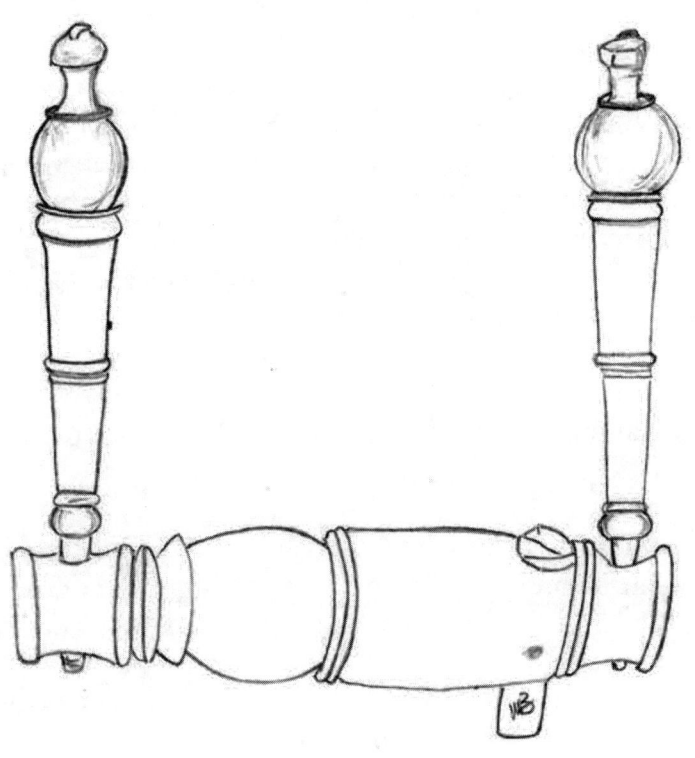

The Maidens

Play Your Drum

Tune: *Congo*

Words & Music copyright © 2010 Corean Bakke
All rights reserved. Admin. Bakken Books

Discovery Penetrates Darkness

With a hymn completed for Easter, Pentecost, Advent, Christmas, and Lent, it was time to write one for Epiphany. This had been a difficult season when it came to choosing words. I was caught between *manifestation*, a word I refused to use,[4] and *aha* which does not lend itself to a hymn text. My new dictionary, after defining the religious meaning of Epiphany, gave a secular definition: "moment of profound insight." [5]

With the deadline approaching for getting an Epiphany hymn written, I took the worrisome project with me to Santa Barbara, California. On a drive exploring nearby vineyards, I asked Ray to tell me a story of when he experienced a moment of profound insight. He told me of sitting in the public library in Fairbanks, Alaska (when he could not get a job), reading *More Light on the Dead Sea Scrolls* by Miller Burrows.[6] In chapter three, page one, paragraph two, he found information that he had been hoping to find for months. He tossed the book in the air and broke the silence by exclaiming, "Alleluia!" The discovery changed his life.

---

[4] Manifestation is not a common word. It must be explained. I was looking for a single word that could express the essence of the season without needing an explanation.

[5] *The Oxford Desk Dictionary and Thesaurus,* 2nd ed., Spark Publishing, NY, 2007.

[6] Miller Burrows, *More Light on the Dead Sea Scrolls*, Viking Press, New York, 1958, p. 39.

Scripture contains stories of sudden insights that changed people's lives. Wise men in the East sighted a star that compelled them to follow. Jesus offered to give a woman *living* water, guaranteed to forever displace thirst. Saul fell to the ground when confronted by a voice and blinding light. Peter was told *three times*, in a dream, to kill and eat forbidden animals.

Martin Luther experienced a moment of profound insight when he discovered in Romans[7] the key to solving his personal frustration: "The just shall live by faith." [8]

Heartened by success for a project so long hampered by lack of words and undeterred by five verses already completed, I proceeded with yet another verse. This last verse of my Epiphany hymn is for those whose moment of profound insight is yet to happen. This verse builds on Jesus' teaching in the Sermon on the Mount: "Seek and ye shall find." [9]

In retrospect, I wonder why it took so long to grasp a working concept for Epiphany. On 27 July 2007, my wistful ambition to write a complete set of hymns for the Church Year was complete. It had taken three years.

---

[7] Roland Bainton, *Here I Stand, A Life of Martin Luther*, Abingdon Press, New York, pp.60,65.

[8] Romans 1:17 KJV

[9] Matthew 7:7 KJV

Discovery Penetrates Darkness

Tune: *Santa Barbara*

Words & Music copyright © 2008 Corean Bakke
All rights reserved. Admin. Bakken Books.

The People Who Walked in Darkness

An Epiphany text from Isaiah would not leave my mind. Each year, once my decorations for the season are in place, a Scripture verse faces me from the kitchen fireplace mantel: "The people that walked in darkness . . ." George Frideric Handel included those words in *Messiah* in 1742, giving them to the bass soloist. The melody takes many turns and twists, imitating the directionless walk of a person stranded in darkness. On the heels of that torturous musical journey, Handel placed hope. He jumped to another verse in Isaiah and wrote a chorus that announces the birth of a Child using one choir section at a time. He gradually involved all voices in an exciting declaration of the names that Child would be called.

I began planning a simple song for cantor and congregation, one that could be used often and easily memorized. The first task was to choose a translation. With the words of Handel's King James English rooted in my memory, I could not stray far. I chose the New King James Version where only a few small changes had been made, removing clutter from the antiquated text.

I divided the two verses into three sections. A cantor sings the first section – about walking in darkness – slowly. The sluggish melody, accompanied by minor chords, imitates how I walk in the dark: cautiously, fearful of falling. After this introduction-like beginning, the congregation announces the birth of a Child in a major key, singing on a single pitch, but at a quicker pace. The final section lists the names the Child will be called. At this point, both melody and rhythm come alive. That section repeats, celebrating the happy energetic ending.

Not until a hymn is used can I consider it completely finished. I need to experience how it works. In this case I wondered whether the opening melody would be impossibly dull and have to be reworked. At the first rehearsal with the cantor, we agreed that a fermata was needed to mark the ending of that section before the congregation entered with a change of key and tempo. Nothing more.

I call this the text that refused to be ignored and demanded a simple musical setting for cantor and congregation.

The result is not a hymn, and yet it deserves a more specialized word than simply *song* or even *Scripture song*. My new dictionary defines *canticle* as "song or chant with a Biblical text," [10] confirming the category suggested by Dr. Hustad. I am pleased to have written a canticle.

---

[10] *The Oxford Desk Dictionary and Thesaurus,* 2nd ed., Spark Publishing, New York, 2007.

The People Who Walked in Darkness

Words: Isaiah 9:2,6
Music copyright © 2010 Corean Bakke
All rights reserved. Admin. Bakken Books.

Lyrics from the New King James Version ®.
Copyright © 1982 Thomas Nelson, Inc.
Used by Permission.

Does Anybody Care

It was time to write a Lenten hymn, something that would fit my definition of the season as a time of testing and struggle. A conversation with a guest came to mind.

One morning at breakfast, with the kitchen filled with students, Nancy accompanied me outside to feed my two cats. I asked a few questions and her story of domestic abuse tumbled out. Over the years, her story had miraculously expanded. Once a desperate mother with three small children, she now traveled the world as an advocate for women and spokesperson on trafficking and domestic violence.

When my husband suggested a tour of First Nation villages on Vancouver Island with Nancy as our guide, I again thought of her story and my need to write a Lenten hymn. I took along a notebook in hopes that an opportunity to ask more questions might arise. While we were riding a ferry, I asked Nancy if she could tell me the words she prayed when trapped in an abusive, frightening marriage.

Back home, I went to the Bookmobile and checked out CDs of singers performing blues. This was a genre I knew little about, apart from a few classically oriented blues written for solo piano. I studied the melodies, lyrics, and supporting accompaniment.

I learned that the words are the most important part of a blues song. The vocal style is declamatory, often using a single repeated pitch for lengthy portions of the song. Very often, the words ask a question. They are words of pain and pathos chanted rather than spoken, chanted rather than sung. Lower tones are used for telling the story of woe. Higher tones are used for emotional venting.

The tempo is slow, giving time for the words of the story to work their way into the listener's heart. Harmony stays out of the way, at times almost acting as a drone. Rhythm holds the song together.

Nancy's prayer became a blues. I sent her a copy of *her* words arranged into three verses and *my* words in a fourth verse.

"Dear Corean, I am so moved, I can barely breathe. You didn't forget. You're a healer. Thank you! Thank you!"

Instead of a hymn, I had written a solo for mezzo voice. We are still looking for soloist and pianist to perform this song in authentic blues style.

Does Anybody Care

Tune: Nancy

Words & Music copyright © 2008 Corean Bakke
All rights reserved. Admin. Bakken Books.

Lament

On the evening of 19 March 2003, I was organist for the Lenten service at my church. A few minutes after the benediction, as people prepared to leave, we were quieted to hear an announcement. US planes were bombing Iraq.

Ray and I drove home with heavy hearts.

Both of us have been to the Middle East. Ray has been there many times, even to Baghdad. We have learned the folly of violent intervention in Muslim countries where retaliation brews for centuries. The consequences were beyond our imagining. This war could destabilize surrounding nations. Lacking knowledge of Christian communities in the Middle East, Americans had neither sorrow nor compassion. Iraq's ancient history is intertwined with biblical history. Few people shared our concerns. We feared for the future of our country

News of the war, reported as remarkable successes, permeated the news. I resolutely refused to celebrate US aggression.

I placed a black and white mosaic tile of two Muslim women on the kitchen fireplace mantel to remind me to pray for the women of Baghdad. It would stay there, no matter the season, until that war came to an end.

With no Lenten hymn yet written and the conflict evolving into bigger and worse devastation, I decided to write about the war. What I had yet to hear was any song of contrition. I strongly felt the need for a prayer of corporate confession: "Lord, have mercy."

One morning before getting out of bed I read Lamentations. I was looking for assistance from Jeremiah, the weeping prophet, who lived through the destruction of Jerusalem, his beloved city. The fifteenth verse of the last chapter furnished words to complete the refrain:

> The joy of our heart has ceased;
> Our dance has turned into mourning.

What did I mourn? With pencil and paper in pocket, handy for writing when thoughts came, I worked in my kitchen, cooking and cleaning.

A houseguest arrived – my first acquaintance with post-traumatic stress disorder in the military. His experience gave me additional motivation.

As I write this story, it is the season of Pentecost 2010. The tile of the two Muslim women remains on my kitchen fireplace mantel.

Ray and I continue to fear for our country.

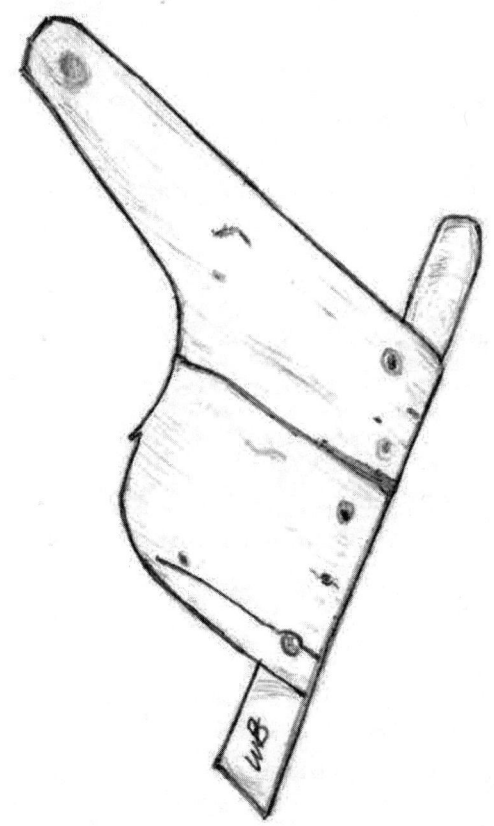

Treadle

Can Anything Separate Us

My first attempt at writing a hymn for Lent, "Does Anybody Care" became a blues solo. My second attempt, "Lament," with its strong language about the war in Iraq, became the most controversial of all my hymns. Neither was suitable for all-around use. I would try a third time.

Part of the problem was my description of Lent as the season of testing: we struggle. At one time I gathered six hymns, choosing one to represent each season of the Church Year. My choice for Lent was the best of them all. "How Firm a Foundation" described testing such as Ray and I have experienced, especially "fiery trials" of verse four. That hymn dates from 1787.

Now searching for hymn models focused on testing, I discovered anew the language of the Afro-American spirituals. However, at a standstill for words and not wanting to come up short a third time, I opened my Contemporary English Version to Romans, chapter 8, verses 35, 38-39. That text is about testing and God's supporting love throughout.

I copied the three-part affirmation of God's love, and in-between inserted the lists of things that could demolish us. The result looked thus:

Can anything separate us from the love of God?[11]

> Trouble, suffering, hard times, hunger, nakedness, danger, death.

I am sure that nothing can separate us from God's love.

> Not life or death, not angels or spirits, not the present or the future, not powers above or powers below.

Nothing in all creation can separate us from God's love. (CEV)

It was a perfectly balanced text! I could hardly wait until the next day to begin setting these words to music for congregation and cantor.

The congregation sings the affirmations twice. The cantor sings each list once. Those melodies are a bit complex and not suitable for congregation.

This canticle is appropriate for any time during the Church Year, but especially for Lent.

---

[11] The American Bible Society granted permission for me to substitute *God* for *Christ* in this line of the text.

Can Anything Separate Us
Based on Romans 8:35,38,39

Music: Corean Bakke
Words: Based on Romans 8:35, 38-39a
Music copyright © 2010 Corean Bakke
All rights reserved. Admin. Bakken Books

CEV text copyright © 2006
American Bible Society. Adapted by permission.

At Dawn They Came

At a worship meeting in January of 2004 with the new interim pastor, we planned through Easter Sunday. His Easter homily would be about the women at the tomb. He needed a Hymn of the Day on that topic.[12] None of us knew of a hymn about the women. He asked me to write one.

All the way home, I thought about this assignment. Two things beckoned me: the strange absence of a hymn about the women, and my concern over lack of creativity for Easter. The Lutheran hymnal in our pew racks has more hymns for Christmas than for Easter. While Easter is the most important date in the Christian calendar, Christmas supersedes it in attention.

I began, while sitting in a chapel listening to a long-winded speaker, by analyzing Easter music in the hymnal. I drew a line down the middle of a sheet of paper: the features to avoid (9), the features to consider (8). For example, I wanted to avoid a march meter and instead, write in a dance meter. I preferred a light-hearted text to pedantic teaching. And for certain, I did not want descending *aleluyas*! That hymnal had nineteen Easter hymns. Five of them modeled the joy and spontaneity I wanted to pursue.

Miriam, sister of Moses and Aaron, led a celebration after the Hebrews successfully crossed the Red Sea. She led the women in dancing and playing

---

[12] In the Lutheran liturgy, the homily (sermon) is followed by a hymn that emphasizes the main point of the homily. It is called the Hymn of the Day.

tambourines.[13] I would write an Easter dance for voices and tambourines.

Because I no longer drive at night, I arrived before nightfall for the February church council meeting. In Washington State that is late afternoon. I walked to the nearby public library and with manuscript paper and the story elements from each Gospel spread in front of me on the table, a narrative hymn took shape. Matthew inspired verse one; Mark, verse two; Luke, verse three; John, verse four. A fifth verse summarized the story.

When the council meeting began at 7:00, all five verses were written and words were in place beneath the notes of a melody. This had never happened to me before. Tinkering with words, melody, and key took a few more days.

When it was ready to share, I e-mailed a friend in Illinois. He asked to see my handwritten hymn and then, offered to format it on his computer software. Thanks to Tony, I had nice copies for my interim pastor (who would quote one line in his homily), the organist, the choir for advance rehearsal, and the congregation.

On Easter Sunday, the congregation at Our Saviour's Lutheran sang my first hymn as the Hymn of the Day.

---

[13] Exodus 15:20

At Dawn They Came

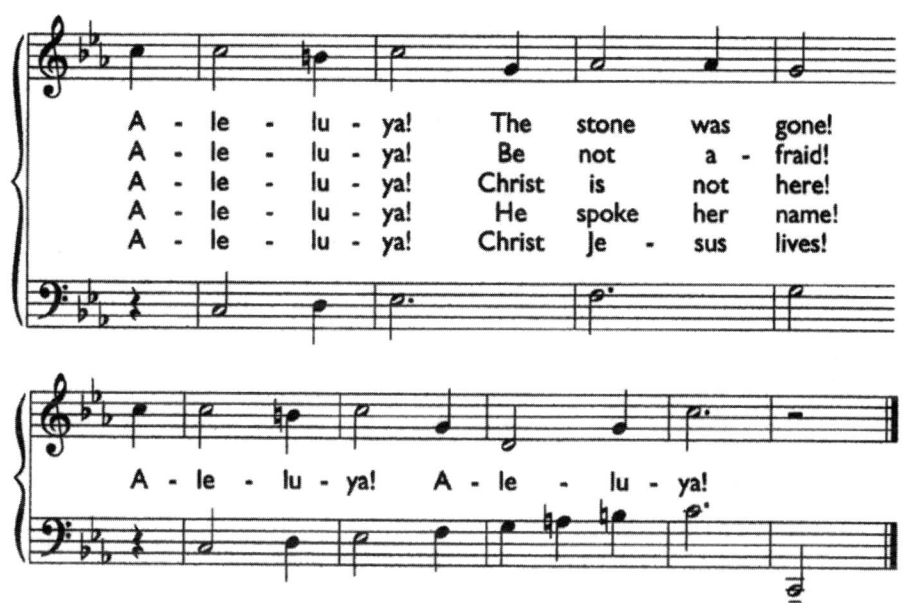

Aleluya

With an Easter season vespers to plan, I searched for a simple Taize song to use. Aside from alleluias written with just that one word for the entire song, I found nothing. I would try to write one.

The choice of words was critical: simple, clear, and to the point. On Easter Sunday I returned to reading *Christianity Rediscovered* by Vincent Donovan.[14] As a missionary to the Masai in Kenya, he tried to strip all cultural baggage from the gospel and present it as simply as possible. I wanted my little song to express the core of the gospel and lean toward a narrative approach, rather than an interpretive approach.

On the first Monday of Easter while weeding raspberries, I sang the newly composed refrain over and over. It had one word, *Aleluya*, used seven times. I have used this spelling ever since putting together an international hymnal. The Spanish spelling, with its economy of letters, is more appealing to me than the traditional alleluia spelling. I would need to get an opinion as to whether my new *"Aleluya"* was too connected to the Taize *"Gloria."* There definitely is a melodic resemblance.

I stayed over night in Bellingham on Tuesday in order to chair a call committee meeting. We had just interviewed a seventh candidate for pastor. My mind woke me early on Wednesday, mulling over the wording for the song. Never again would I leave an

---

[14] Vincent J. Donovan, *Christianity Rediscovered*, 2nd ed., Orbis Books, Maryknoll, NY, 1982.

unfinished song at home. It needs to be with me as I evaluate the words.

By Thursday I had a full set of words and wanted Ray to see them. I e-mailed them to China where he was traveling with students from Bakke Graduate University.[15] On the second Thursday of Easter, I made a handwritten copy of my song, ready to xerox and give to the cantor. I mailed a copy for musical critique.

We sang the new Easter song on 7 May 2006 with a cantor singing the verses and the congregation singing the refrain. From the first note, they sang as if they already knew it!

Not until later did the critique arrive from Dr. Hustad, suggesting a different placement of the second syllable of the final *Aleluya*. Moving that syllable from count four to count six greatly improved the soaring melody as it approached the final measure. As for the melodic resemblance, it was too slight to worry about.

My little Easter song, as I call it, has been used at vespers every Easter season since it was written.

---

[15] Bakke Graduate University is located in Seattle, Washington.

Aleluya

God be-came man in Beth-le-hem.
Wit-nessed by all, fol-lowed by some,
Af-ter three days Je-sus a-rose!
Life con-quered death. Hope hushed des-pair.

Je-sus his name, his mis-sion plain:
God in the flesh made a big stir.
E-vil could not main-tain con-trol.
Joy dis-placed fear as friends be-lieved.

preach-ing and teach-ing and heal-ing the sick.
En-e-mies plot-ted to put him to death.
With great a-maze-ment the truth be-came known.
Je-sus be-came proof that God al-ways wins!

Words & Music copyright © 2008 Corean Bakke
All rights reserved. Admin. Bakken Books

Do Not Leave This Place

After the success of my Easter hymn, I was motivated to try again. With Pentecost coming in fifty days, perhaps another success was possible.

A week and a half after Easter, I had yet to begin. On a council day at my Lutheran church, when I often scheduled other appointments in town, I arrived at the Imaging Center one hour early. With Bible, notebook, and pencil in hand, I intended to begin another narrative hymn. After carefully reading Acts, chapter two, I realized that this was not going to be easy or quick.

I arrived at church early for the council meeting and used the time to analyze the Pentecost hymns in our two pew hymnals. In *Lutheran Book of Worship*,[16] our principal hymnal, I found five hymns in the Pentecost section. I found nine in our supplementary hymnal, *With One Voice*,[17] which contained hymns collected from other cultures and hymns newly written.

A Nigerian call-and-response hymn, written for congregation and leader, caught my attention. I would write for cantor, choir, and congregation.

A week later it had taken shape as a three-part musical drama. The cantor set the scene for each of

---

[16] *Lutheran Book of Worship*, Augsburg Publishing House, Minneapolis, and Board of Publication, Lutheran Church in America, Philadelphia, 1978.

[17] *With One Voice*, Augsburg Fortress, Minneapolis, 1995.

the five verses. The choir extended each scene. After each verse, the congregation sang a response, always the same one.

With Pentecost Sunday still three weeks away, I had time to hand-write a clean copy[18] and deliver it to the church office. The choir needed advance copies to learn its single musical line that begins in unison and splits into parts. The secretary would decide how best to present this hymn in the worship folder without confusing the congregation. The organ would participate only with the cantor and the congregation. The choir would sing *a cappella*.

People in the congregation were enthusiastic. They could listen to cantor and choir and follow the story without having to focus their attention on complicated music. Their part was simple and short.

Ray paid special attention to how the words of the congregational response functioned at the end of each verse, and approved. He liked the three-part structure, called it Trinitarian.

With successful hymns for two seasons of the church year, I wondered whether I should keep writing. Four seasons remained. Why not?

---

[18] Although I had purchased Sibelius software for formatting music on my computer, I lacked the expertise needed to deal with this complex song.

Do Not Leave This Place

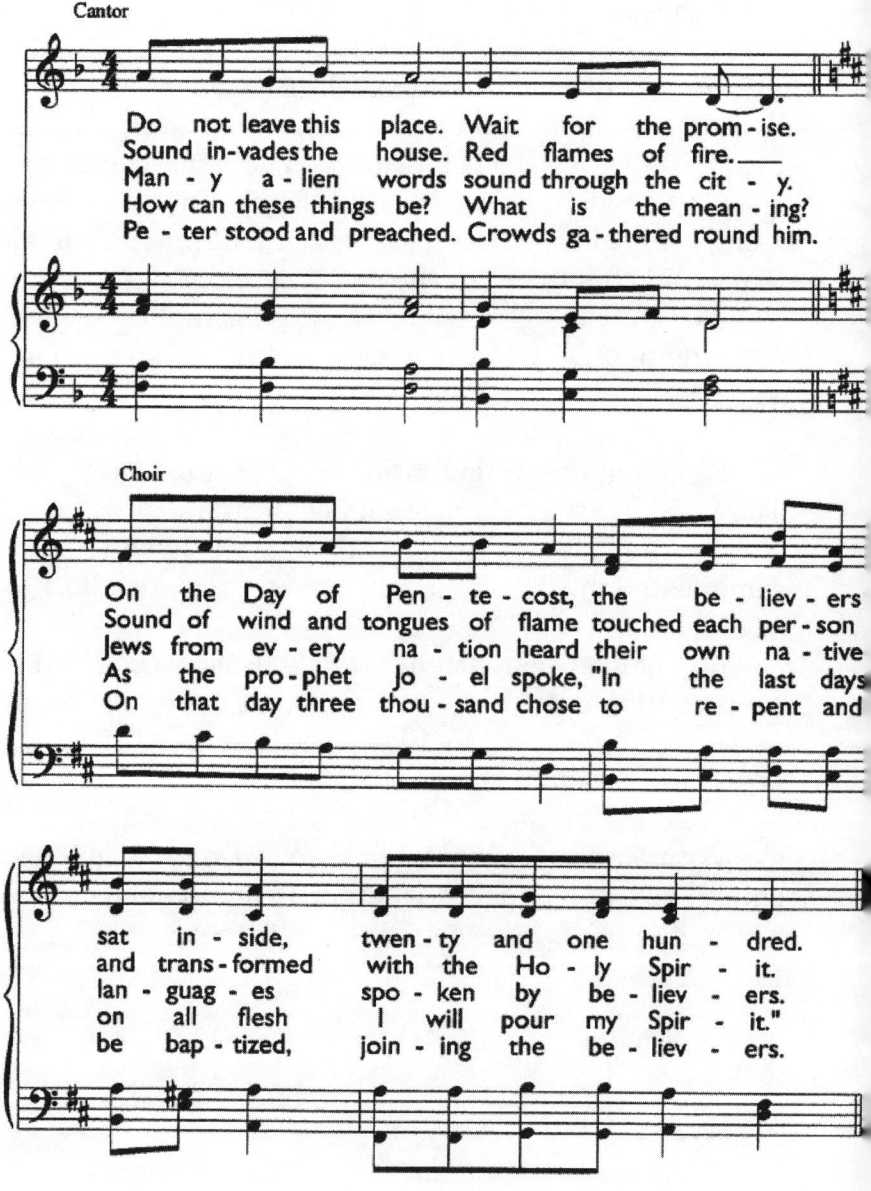

Words & Music copyright © 2010 Corean Bakke
All rights reserved. Admin. Bakken Books.

Comforting, encouraging, teaching and empowering, come, Holy Spirit, come!

Comforting, Encouraging

Collaboration with creative people produces surprises. Although I have learned to expect surprises, they catch me unexpectedly. Working with a composer whose skills and creativity far surpass mine was bound to result in surprises.

Tony Payne lives and works in Wheaton, Illinois, near Chicago. I live and work at Bakken, the home my husband and I – with the help of countless friends and family – made in northwest Washington State, near Acme. When Tony and I first worked together compiling a hymnal, the fax machine was newly available. Because that hymnal needed to include music from other cultures and languages, it was amazing and exciting to discover that I could receive music from the other side of the world in my little attic office.

Twenty years later, I continue to marvel over ever more advanced technology that permits partners to live and work thousands of miles apart.

As editor of *Aleluya: Singing the Church Year*, Tony engraved each song – notes and words – and e-mailed the PDF file to me. The first song to arrive had two treble clefs instead of one. The extra clef was for the *echo* part he had added, enabling a secondary group of singers to begin one measure behind the primary group of singers. This delightful surprise opened new possibilities for what was intended to be a congregational refrain. His echo addition transformed my refrain into a complete song with its own title: "Comforting, Encouraging," a song about the Holy Spirit.

The Season of Pentecost extends for half the year, from Pentecost Sunday in late spring to Advent on the final Sunday of November. It is such a long season that the coming and continuing presence of the Holy Spirit gets lost. Here was a short song with echo that could be easily included in worship to keep that awareness alive.

This setting of the song aligned it with the current trend in contemporary worship to sing simple, short songs more than once. In order for the echo to complete its role in the song, repetition is necessary.

Simple short songs are easily memorized. They go home with you and sing themselves over and over in your mind. Radio used that phenomenon to great advantage by airing musical ads. They stuck in people's minds. Considerably in advance of radio, Martin Luther recognized the possibility of teaching through hymns. The theology people sang did not remain in the church pews. It went home with them.

I am indebted to Tony for recognizing the potential in my simple melody, for spending time writing an echo that can be easily sung, and for expanding a refrain into this short song about the Holy Spirit.

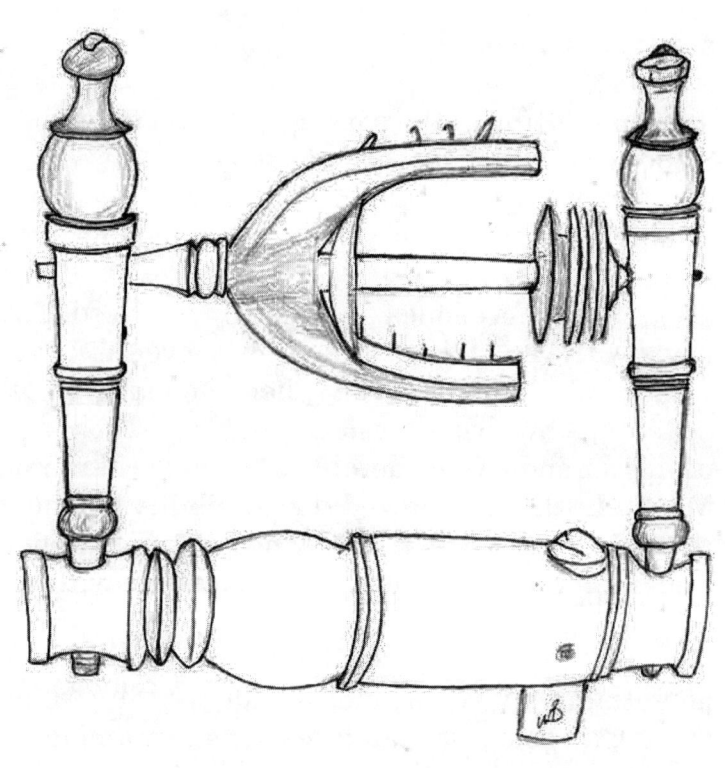

The Mother of All

Comforting, Encouraging

Tune: *Payne*

Words & Music copyright © 2010 Corean Bakke
All rights reserved. Admin. Bakken Books.

Holy Spirit, Come to This Place

I was asked to plan morning devotions for the Board of Regents of Bakke Graduate University. This international group of twenty women and men would meet at our home in September for its annual retreat.

For me, planning any kind of worship begins by identifying the season of the Church Year. The regents would come during the season of Pentecost – the season of empowerment, when we grow.

The mission statement at my Lutheran church included words about the Holy Spirit: "By the grace of God, we at Our Saviour's Lutheran Church are filled with the Holy Spirit and respond to God's love by sharing the Good News with our friends and neighbors. We go into our community and world to make a difference in the name of Jesus."

Cancer had stricken four significant people in my life: two members of the bell choir that I direct, a niece, and the best friend of our youngest son. My daily prayers included them as they struggled with chemotherapy and radiation. In each case, their fear could easily be discerned over hundreds and thousands of miles that separated us.

For years I debated the childhood theology of the little prayer song: "Into my heart, into my heart. Come into my heart, Lord Jesus . . ." I had trouble reconciling that prayer with Jesus' words to his disciples: that he was going to leave them, but he was not going to abandon them. He had a plan, a gift for them. The Holy Spirit would come. Then they would be better off than when Jesus was with them. They would be empowered in extraordinary ways and reminded of forgotten things he had taught them.

With these intermingling thoughts, a prayer to the Holy Spirit began taking shape. I wanted to write a prayer that I could sing when frightened and fearful of what might happen; a prayer that I could sing when confused about what to do, when decisions had to be made, when life handed me unexpected challenges.

Putting aside my distance from a word used too often, I included *love* in the third verse. A friend worked with me, via e-mail from Banda Aceh, Indonesia, to grasp the essence of his volunteer efforts following the devastating tsunami of January 2005.

While I think of the first verse for the cancer-stricken people in my life in the summer of 2008, the second verse for myself, and the third verse for Our Saviour's, this hymn is offered for all who would pray to the Holy Spirit.

Holy Spirit, Come to This Place

Tune: *Banda Aceh*

Copyright © 2010 Corean Bakke
All rights reserved. Admin. Bakken Books.

God Creator Fashioned Beauty

The Trinity Tree has been significant from the first day Ray stepped foot on the place we now call Bakken. The trunk of this cedar divided into three sections at the base, making it grow as a three-branched candelabra. Ray built a protective box around it. I planted white heather.

Every person who comes to visit is taken to see the Trinity Tree. It inspired our mission statement. It grounds the spirituality of this place.

> We want Bakken to be a place of beauty
> to reflect God our Creator.
> We want Bakken to be a place of peace
> to reflect God our Redeemer.
> We want Bakken to be a place of transformation
> to reflect God our Helper.

It finally occurred to me that I should write a hymn about the Trinity and include the words of our mission statement.

Verse one describes the Pacific Northwest, including Bakken. It recalls the garden of Eden and God's task for Adam: he was to dress it and keep it.[19] Ray and I feel called to this place, not only to enjoy it and carry out our ministry from this place, but to carefully take care of these nearly twelve acres. Those antiquated words from my youthful reading of Genesis come to mind as I work outside tending my gardens.

---

[19] Genesis 2:15 KJV

Verse two celebrates our place of quiet. We moved to a mountainside from inner city Chicago near Lake Michigan, where planes approaching O'Hare Airport – one of the three busiest airports in the world – circled for landing. The only overhead noise we hear now is an occasional helicopter or small private plane. Verse two also alludes to tensions within relationships on this mountain.

Verse three is about God our Helper. The prominence of the Trinity Tree and formulation of this mission statement have resulted in greater consciousness of the Holy Spirit. Bakken has transformed our lives. Friends ask whether we miss Chicago. We surprise even ourselves by saying no. Guests have told us stories of transformation resulting from their visits here. These changes are beyond our doing. We bow in humble adoration.

I chose f-sharp minor, a key of three sharps, to symbolize the Trinity.

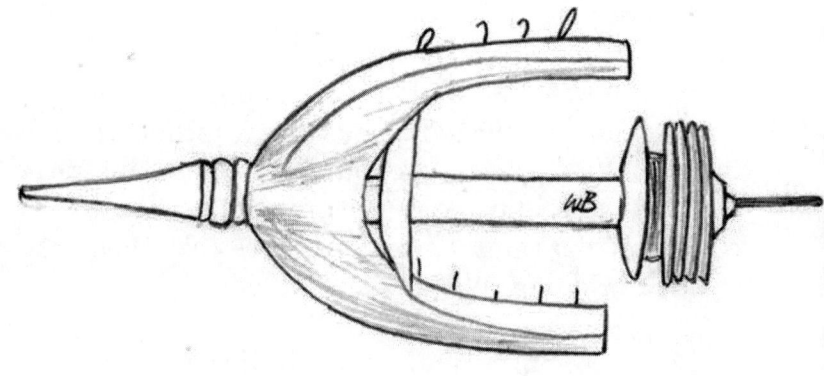

The Flyer

God Creator Fashioned Beauty

Tune: Bakken

Words & Music copyright © 2010 Corean Bakke
All rights reserved. Admin. Bakken Books.

Once in the Village of Nazareth

I had never thought of writing a hymn about Mary even though Ray and I have a special outdoor place we named Mary of Nazareth Grotto. I told my Bible study group of the request from my pastor friend and invited them to help me. We had been studying the women in Luke's Gospel, but skipped over Mary, reserving her story for a time closer to Christmas. I requested that next week we go back and study Mary.

This group of six women meets together weekly. They have known each other for most of their lives and raised their children together. They are well read, insightful, and not timid about expressing their opinions. I joined their group as a new arrival in the community and have come to respect their wisdom and counsel. They had helped me on earlier writing projects. When I brought them the rough draft of a Bible study discussion guide titled *Time to Talk in Church About HIV and AIDS*, they used it as the study for the group. Working slowly and carefully, they sent me home after each session with red markings all over my copy, of corrections to make.

I searched for hymn texts already written about Mary and took a Roman Catholic and Episcopalian hymnal to the next Bible study. I read those hymns of devotion, written about Mary as a saint, to the group. I wanted to write a hymn about Mary as a person.

We read aloud Luke, chapters one and two, selecting the verses about Mary. With pencil and paper in hand, I listened as they talked and lifted out of the narrative concepts that described Mary as a person, Mary as a parent.

Two weeks later I brought a first verse – text and music – and made notes of their comments:

> Why is it in a minor key? It's written too high for me to sing.
> Where is this going? Is it for Christmas? Or is it about the passion and resurrection?
> It cannot have lots of verses because song leaders will leave out most of them.

We made a list of things to include from the narrative. I added four more verses and received more comments:

> I'm glad it's not twelve verses long!
> It ends by connecting her story with ours.
> *Fled* is not going on vacation, or moving, or relocating.
> 'In the night' expresses the urgency and danger.
> 'Interceded at Cana's feast . . .' How did Mary expect Jesus to solve the problem, if this was his first miracle?

I am greatly indebted to this group of women. They unflinchingly assist me with projects.

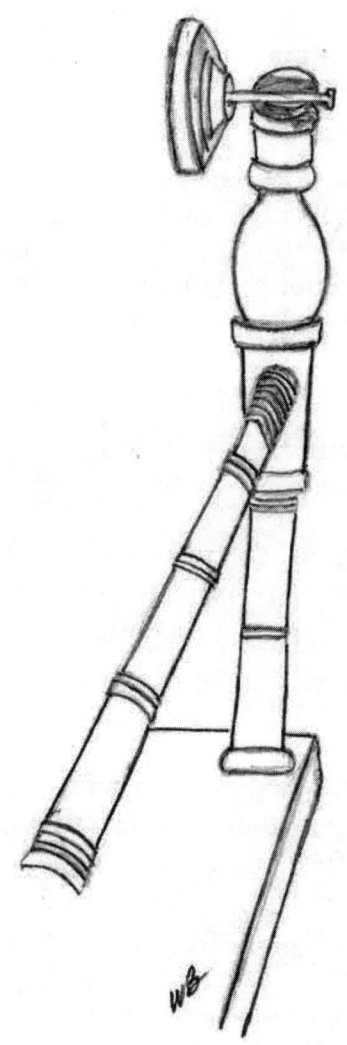

Right Maiden

Once in the Village of Nazareth

Tune: Acme

Words & Music copyright © 2010 Corean Bakke
All rights reserved. Admin. Bakken Books.

When Will Jesus Come

A conversation with the organist/choirmaster at my church prompted this song. In October he talked through the seasonal expectation for Advent – that the choir and congregation not sing Christmas music until Christmas Eve. He made clear his displeasure with the music available for Sundays of Advent. Impulsively I spoke up and asked if I were to write something, such as a simple carol, should it be for congregation or choir? He chose for the choir.

I already knew of his discomfort with dark and somber Advent music for *four* Sundays in contrast to a wealth of beloved music for *two* Sundays during Christmas. I had written an arrangement for bell choir and voice on the tune "Greensleeves." This melody is used in our hymnal for the Christmas carol "What Child is This." I wrote the soprano part as a vocalise (without words) and titled it with the name of the tune, thereby avoiding the Christmas words. Our pastor gave his approval for including it on the fourth Sunday of Advent.

The first two verses of "What Child is This" ask a question. The refrain gives the answer. That textual format gave me an idea for constructing an Advent carol. I would write a question-and-answer musical dialogue for the choir. The women would ask questions that have been asked for many centuries, in many countries. The men would answer with Jesus' words.

I worked with a red-letter edition of the New Testament and consulted several translations, primarily the New Revised Standard Version, and the

New King James. A simple word change in the translation can make a big difference in fitting text to music. In some cases, fitting required editing the biblical text by leaving out words or rearranging them.

Not until writing this story did the answer in verse one raise a personal question: Had I confused an imagined answer with an authentic verse in Scripture? Revelation 22:20 reads: "I am coming soon." But I had inserted an extra word *very*. The music needed the extra word! An energetic search through all of my translations finally legitimatized my wording for the men's answer. The Moffatt translation[20] of that verse reads: "I am coming very soon."

The answer in verse two involved changes. Matthew 5:14 reads "You are the light of the world." I changed that answer to read: "You are light for all the world." Even though the literal reading contains the same number of syllables as my altered version, the original grammatical construction is not metrically suitable for the music.

In verse three, "Do not be afraid" fit perfectly. Jesus is quoted using that phrase seventeen times in the four Gospels. I had not been aware of that frequency until told by the pastor who drew me into hymn writing. In Mark 5:36 (NKJ), this phrase is followed by "only believe." I omitted *only*.

---

[20] James Moffatt, *The Bible, A New Translation*, Harper & Brothers Publishers, New York, 1922.

In verse four, the answer reads: "I am with you to the end." Matthew 28:20 (NRSV) reads: "I am with you always, to the end of the age."

Verse five departs from the established question and answer format, and begins with the men quoting Jesus from four different scriptural locations. These are the most edited of all the quotes.

Therefore watch and pray. Luke 21:36
You know not the time. Matthew 24:42
Coming with great power: Mark 13: 26
When you least expect: Matthew 24:44

In verse five the women respond: "We repeat creation's plea." This is a brief allusion to Romans 8:22 that reads: "For we know that the whole creation groans and labors with birth pangs . . . ." (NKJ)

The women continue with words from Revelation 22:20: "Come, Lord Jesus, quickly come." *Quickly*, found in the King James, is translated *soon* in the New Revised Standard Version.

This Advent carol, with timely questions and ancient answers and placed in a simple unison musical setting, was sung *a cappella* on the last Sunday of Advent 2010.

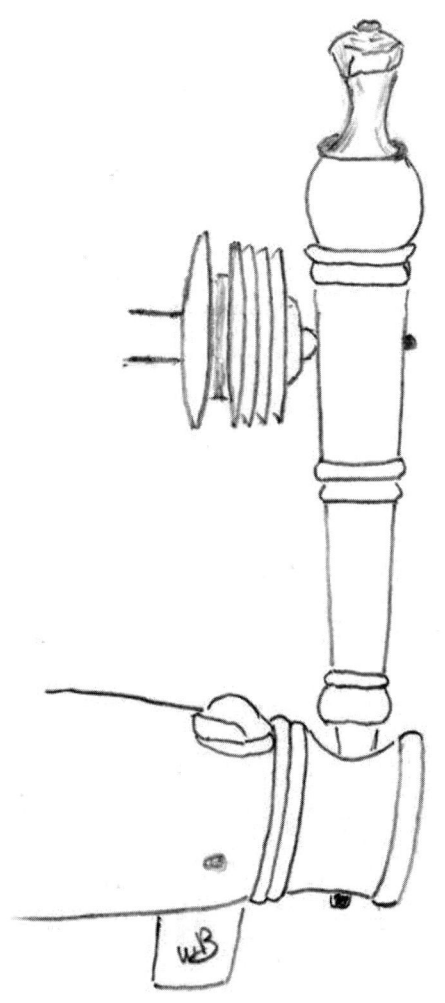

Right Maiden
Mother of All

When Will Jesus Come

1. When will Jesus come and renew the world? Days and months and years go by and yet he does not come. You forget the words he said: I am coming very soon.
2. When will justice win over lies and greed: no one hungry, no one homeless, no one destitute? You forget the words he said: You are light for all the world.
3. When will evil end and the violence cease? Fear increases. Threats grow stronger. Where shall we go hide? You forget the words he said: Do not be afraid. Believe!
4. When will crying cease and emotions heal: no more sickness, no more dying, no more broken heart? You forget the words he said: I am with you to the end.

Words & Music copyright © 2010 Corean Bakke
All rights reserved. Admin. Bakken Books.

SCRIPTURE INDEX

Genesis
1 and 2	God Creator Fashioned Beauty	73

II Chronicles
7:14	Lament	45

Joel
2:28-29	Do Not Leave This Place	60

Isaiah
7:14	Jesus Christ, We Sing to You	14
9:2,6	The People Who Walked	36
12:2	Once in the Village of Nazareth	77

Lamentations
5:15	Lament	45

Psalm
27:14	Jesus Christ, We Sing to You	14
37:3-5	Once in the Village of Nazareth	77
123:3	Does Anybody Care	40
123:3	Lament	45

Proverbs
3:5	Once in the Village of Nazareth	77

Matthew
1	Aleluya	56
1:23	Jesus Christ, We Sing to You	14
2:1-12	Discovery Penetrates Darkness	32
2:1-23	Rome Gave Orders	22
2:10-11	Play Your Drum	29
5:13-16	Holy Spirit, Come to This Place	69
5: 14-16	When Will Jesus Come	82

5:43-48	God Creator Fashioned Beauty	73
7:7-8	Discovery Penetrates Darkness	32
16:18, 24-26	Jesus Christ, We Sing to You	14
17:15	Does Anybody Care	40
24:42, 44	When Will Jesus Come	82
27:62-28:8	Aleluya	56
28:1-10	At Dawn They Came	52

Mark

13:26, 32-36	When Will Jesus Come	82
16:1-8	At Dawn They Came	52

Luke

1:26-31	Rome Gave Orders	22
1:26-38	Once in the Village of Nazareth	77
1:46-53	The Breath of My Life	18
1:52-53	When Will Jesus Come	82
2	Aleluya	56
2:1-20	Play Your Drum	29
2:1-51	Rome Gave Orders	22
2:1-51	Once in the Village of Nazareth	77
4:16-19	Aleluya	56
6:27-36	God Creator Fashioned Beauty	73
21:34-35a	When Will Jesus Come	82
24:1-12	At Dawn They Came	52
24:13-35	Holy Spirit, Come to This Place	69
24:13-48	Aleluya	56
24:30-35	Jesus Christ We Sing to You	14

John

2:1-11	Once in the Village of Nazareth	77
4:5-42	Discovery Penetrates Darkness	32
4:42	Play Your Drum	29
11:45-53	Aleluya	56
14:12	Comforting, Encouraging	65
14:15-26	Holy Spirit, Come to This Place	69

14:15-26	God Creator Fashioned Beauty	73
14:27	God Creator Fashioned Beauty	73
15:26	Comforting, Encouraging	65
16:7-15	Comforting, Encouraging	65
19:16-30	Once in the Village of Nazareth	77
20:1-18	At Dawn They Came	52
20:24-29	Aleluya	56

Acts

1:4-5	Do Not Leave This Place	60
1:6-14	Once in the Village of Nazareth	77
1:8	Comforting, Encouraging	65
1:8	God Creator Fashioned Beauty	73
2:1-41	Do not Leave This Place	60
2:1-41	God Creator Fashioned Beauty	73
2:1-41	Holy Spirit, Come to This Place	69
2:1-42	Once in the Village of Nazareth	77
9:1-29	Discovery Penetrates Darkness	32
10:1-48	Discovery Penetrates Darkness	32
18:9-10	Play Your Drum	29

Romans

1:17	Discovery Penetrates Darkness	32
8:20-22	When Will Jesus Come	82
8:35,38-39	Can Anything Separate Us	48

I Corinthians

15:3-4	Aleluya	56
15:25-26	Aleluya	56

Galatians

1:3	God Creator Fashioned Beauty	73
1:3	Play Your Drum	29

Ephesians
2:14, 17	God Creator Fashioned Beauty	73
2:14, 17	Play Your Drum	29

I Timothy
1:2b	Does Anybody Care	40
1:2b	God Creator Fashioned Beauty	73
1:2b	Lament	45

Titus
3:6	Play Your Drum	29

I Peter
5:7	Does Anybody Care	40

I John
4:14	Play Your Drum	29

Revelation
22:20	When Will Jesus Come	82

SEASONAL INDEX

Advent

Jesus Christ, We Sing to You	14
The Breath of My Life	18

Christmas

Rome Gave Orders	22
Play Your Drum	29

Epiphany

Discovery Penetrates Darkness	32
The People Who Walked in Darkness	36

Lent

Does Anybody Care	40
Lament	45
Can Anything Separate Us	48

Easter

At Dawn They Came	52
Aleluya	56

Pentecost

Do Not Leave This Place	60
Comforting, Encouraging	65
Holy Spirit, Come to This Place	69
God Creator Fashioned Beauty[21]	73
Once in the Village of Nazareth[22]	77
When Will Jesus Come[23]	82

---

[21] Trinity Sunday – 2nd Sunday of Pentecost
[22] Mary, Mother of Our Lord – August 15
[23] Christ the King – Last Sunday of the Church Year

TITLE INDEX

Aleluya 56

At Dawn They Came 52

Can Anything Separate Us 48

Comforting, Encouraging 65

Discovery Penetrates Darkness 32

Do Not Leave This Place 60

Does Anybody Care 40

God Creator Fashioned Beauty 73

Holy Spirit, Come to This Place 69

Jesus Christ, We Sing to You 14

Lament 45

Once in the Village of Nazareth 77

Play Your Drum 29

Rome Gave Orders 22

The Breath of My Life 18

The People Who Walked in Darkness 36

When Will Jesus Come 82

TUNE INDEX

Acme   77

Bakken   73

Banda Aceh   69

Berry   52

Congo   29

Herod   22

Iraq   45

Katrina   14

Nancy   40

Santa Barbara   32